T0132026

PROFESSOR LOSES HIS JOY

By
Thomas Weatherspoon

Professor Loses His Joy

iUniverse books may be ordered through booksellers or by contacting:

iUniverse
1663 Liberty Drive
Bloomington, IN 47403
www.iuniverse.com
844-349-9409

ISBN: 978-1-6632-4355-3 (sc)
ISBN: 978-1-6632-4356-0 (e)

Library of Congress Control Number: 2022914199

Also by Thomas Weatherspoon
Professor's Path
Professor Has A Goal
Professor Finds The Perfect Gift
Path to Magic 19 Principles of Transformation

Print information available on the last page.

iUniverse rev. date: 08/04/2022

Professor T returned from school and
walked straight to his room.

His Mom noticed immediately his quiet state of gloom.

She knocked softly at his door, making
sure that things were right.

He asked that he be left alone, then sadly said goodnight.
This was not like her son who came home everyday, with a
story of his new discoveries he uncovered while at play.

She knew there was a problem so she called up to his school,
and spoke to the Principal to see if things were cool.

She said, "Professor T got in an argument, while
playing with friends outside, but it never once
got physical and none of them had lied."

She made the kids apologize and end their talk as friends, but
that Professor didn't talk much after, or even smile again.

She didn't know what started it but it had to do with race,
some of the kids were poking fun about features of his face.

What started as a joke somehow grew ugly, and the
kids all said hurtful things and did so laughingly.

She felt they had resolved it and that's why she didn't
call, but tomorrow would address it all in assembly hall.

By the time that she hung up, Mr. Moore was walking in, he greeted her with a warm hello and a kiss upon her chin.

"Where is Professor?" he asked. "How did practice go today? I know he's got a million things to ask me about his play." Mom replied, "He's not feeling well, things didn't go his way. He argued with some kids at school about the negative things they say.

He went upstairs straight to his room and hasn't come out since.

"I think you should go talk to him cause things were kind of tense." His Dad went upstairs to see about his son, he could imagine how sad he was and how this wasn't very fun.

His Dad asked Professor softly if they could go outside, to play a little catch because he needed exercise.

Professor grabbed his ball and glove as they headed for the door. Then Mom gave his Dad a wink, cause that's what Dad's are for.

"I heard you had a problem on the playground
at school today, that the kids were making fun
of you while you guys were out at play?"

Professor tossed the ball right back, and said,
"They were really mean! One minute we were
playing, then they all began to scream.

At first I thought they were joking because they
were all my friends, then they started joking
how I was different from all of them."

Professor's Dad threw the ball but, this time really high,
so high he had to shield the sun to focus on the fly.

He reached his hand up high so the ball would meet the glove,
but then he had to turn his head from the sun there up above.

He caught the ball anyway, even though he
couldn't look, and the accomplishment made him
smile, because of the talent that it took.

His Father cheered loudly, as he approached his son,
"Wow, that was a great catch, probably your best one!"

Professor T smiled and laughed as his Dad wrapped him in his
arms. Because this was his safest place if he ever felt alarmed.
"Professor you must understand, even though you're a little boy,
people can be cruel at times, but they must never steal your
Joy! The only way they can do that is if you participate. Taking
the uncaring things they say and adding to them more weight.
Because those kids called you names, doesn't make them true.
They just have the need to feel they are better than you.

The cruel things that people do or say can
never change this fact. That all of us are God's
greatest magic in life's big magic act."

His Dad then lifted Professor's head and pointed toward the
sun. "The world that God created he made for everyone!"

With that Professor smiled, as bright as the evening sun, and it
made him feel so much better he forgot what they had done.

"That's the way Professor!" His Dad exclaimed. "There's no way if you release your Joy that you can ever feel the same.

See, your Joy is like the sun Professor, it is always there, but if you allow those clouds to hide it, you will eventually feel despair. Then when the sun comes out, you'll feel good again but this slowly becomes the condition on which your happiness depends. Eventually you will only be happy when the sun is out. The times that it's behind the clouds, you then, will begin to doubt.

Your joy, just like the sun, is always here to stay. No matter what the sky looks like, or what the people say.

You be happy knowing, you will always be OK, that regardless of the condition, your Joy is your sunny day."

They played and laughed together until the sun set, and as the two walked inside, his Dad said, "Don't forget!"

"Forget what?" Professor asked, as he closed the door behind. "That both your Joy and your happiness are the permanent kind."

Joy and happiness are what your spirit's made of. To
make things really simple, we just call it love.

That's why you're making magic because your tools are always
there, they forever live inside of you, deep inside somewhere."

Mr. Moore pointed to his son's heart and kissed him on the cheek.
"Now, do your homework, and take a bath, but don't forget to
eat!" As Professor climbed into bed, his Mom came to tuck him in.

"Mom, do you think it will make a difference
if I share my Joy with them."

"Most likely it will son, cause they all want to be happy too,
so go and share your Joy, but let none of this change you.

Goodnight my magic man," and with that they kissed goodnight.

Professor fell off to a peaceful sleep
knowing he would be all right.

The next day in school, the students met in the hall. Then herded into the gymnasium to answer the assembly call.

While the children took their seats, she called a few by name and had them come stand by her, to help her with this game.

In the center of the floor, she had the students stand. Then asked the crowd, "What makes them different?" Then the children raised their hands.

One after another they pointed out the difference. Race, gender, height and weight, their overall appearance.

"Now what makes them all the same?" As the students began to shout, "They're Human, They go to this school, They live here, Without air they'll all pass out!"

They all began to laugh and cheer as the Principal hushed the crowd. "You guys won't be able to hear me, if you continue to be this loud.

Those are all good points and all of them are true. Though we all are different, we are very similar too.

We all laugh, feel pain, fear and sometimes even cry. We feel happy, get our feelings hurt and though we're not supposed to, lie.

It's those things we have in common that allow us to build a bond, with the people we call friends and those we are most fond."

Suddenly the band played out and they all began
to sing, the children belted out their school
song and laughed at the funny things.

Professor T and his friends made up outside at lunch. Though they had they're troubles, they were a very tight nit bunch. Professor was truly happy that everything worked out but would never let his friends again, put his Joy in doubt.

As the last bell rang the kids all headed home. Professor T was the last to leave as he headed out alone.

Suddenly his named was called, as the Principal walked his way.

She asked him how the day worked out and if he felt OK. "Yes," he replied, "We're all friends again. But I have to get to practice now before it all begins."

Professor began to walk away then turned to speak again. "I learned as we played today, it's our differences that make us friends.

And the reason's that we're the same, well you forgot just one.

No matter what our differences, we all share the same sun."

THE END

Printed in the United States
by Baker & Taylor Publisher Services